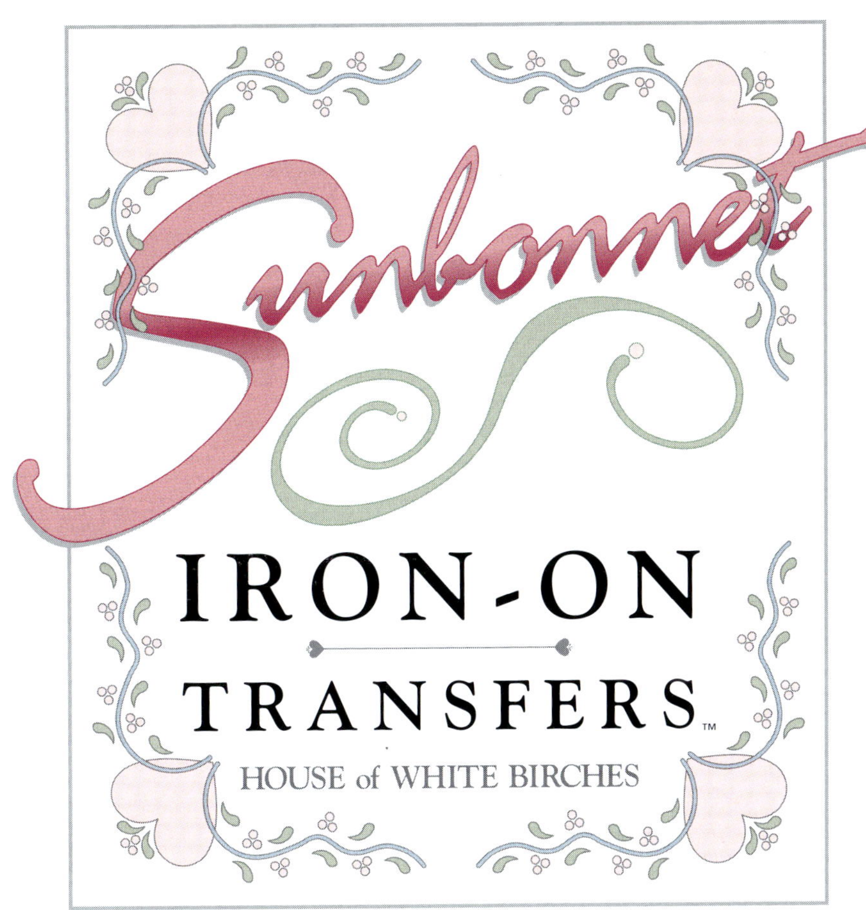

Designs by Barbara Price

Edited by Jeanne Stauffer

Sunbonnet Iron-On Transfers

Editor: Jeanne Stauffer

Project Editor: Beth Wheeler

Copy Editor: Cathy Reef

Photography: Tammy Christian, Nora Elsesser

Photography Assistants: Linda Quinlan, Arlou Wittwer

Production Manager: Vicki Macy

Cover Design: Dan Kraner

Project Book Design/Production: Ronda Bollenbacher

Book Design/Production: Barb Knepple

Graphic Illustrations: Dana Brotherton, Miriam Zacharias

Traffic Coordinator: Sandra Beres

Production Assistants: Carol Dailey, Cheryl Lynch

Publishers: Carl H. Muselman, Arthur K. Muselman

Chief Executive Officer: John Robinson

Marketing Director: Scott Moss

Editorial Director: Vivian Rothe

Production Director: Scott Smith

Printed in the United States of America

First Printing: 1997

Library of Congress Number: 97-72867

ISBN: 1-882138-29-5

Every effort has been made to ensure the accuracy and completeness of the instructions in this book. However, we cannot be responsible for human error or for the results when using materials other than those specified in the instructions, or for variations in individual work.

Cover project: *Tea for Two*, page 92, is modeled by Kim Rife from Charmaine Model Agency, Fort Wayne, Ind., at Swiss Heritage Village, Berne, Ind.

Crafting Fun With Sunbonnet Sue

Sunbonnet Sue has been charming generations of crafters and quilters since she first appeared around the turn of the century, almost 100 years ago.

Bertha L. Corbett Melcher, the "Mother of the Sunbonnet Babies," drew her first design to prove to her artist friends that even a faceless figure could be expressive. Her design so captured the interest of her day that she produced a book and a children's primer. She also became a popular guest on the lecture and vaudeville circuit. The Sunbonnet Babies were often seen in advertising and promotional material, holiday greeting cards and postcards. Eventually, Bertha turned her concept into a popular comic strip.

Sunbonnet Sue is just as popular today. Crafters and quilters are adding Sunbonnet characters to their projects. Their appeal is universal. Because the Sunbonnet faces are not seen, no ethnic or national characteristics show.

Barbara Price is the designer of all 101 fascinating Sunbonnet designs in this versatile craft book. Barbara has always liked the old-fashioned, heartwarming look of Sunbonnet Sue, and several years ago she decided to design a sweatshirt for herself using a Sunbonnet character. She began selling Sunbonnet sweatshirts in a local quilt shop and soon created packets selling her designs because she couldn't keep up with requests for them.

With publication of this iron-on transfer book, Barbara has returned to her first love of drawing Sunbonnet designs. She has created designs for all those everyday and special occasions that take place all year long, beginning with Sue ice-skating in January and ending with her kissing under the mistletoe. You'll find a special design for every month and every day of the week, as well as many holidays. Barbara has also drawn several designs depicting some of her favorite pastimes—sewing, gardening and teatime.

You'll enjoy creating your own keepsake craft and quilting projects with these delightful full-of-memories designs.

Table of Contents

Page 11

Page 76

Page 45

Page 23

Page 50

Page 101

Page 13

General Instructions

Transferring Designs

Determine the best temperature setting for your iron and length of time needed for a good transfer by using the test transfer.

Transferring Onto Fabric

To transfer the chosen design onto fabric for painting, cut the desired iron-on transfer out of the book and place face-down onto a clean, light fabric surface. Be sure that the fabric has been washed and dried without fabric softener.

Place hot, dry iron flat on the transfer for five seconds. Do not move iron around. Pick up iron and place on another area of transfer until all areas have been ironed. Lift corner of paper to ensure proper transfer of design.

Transferring Onto Paper

To transfer the chosen design onto paper for painting or embellishment with colored pencils, markers, watercolor paints, etc., cut desired iron-on transfer out of the book and place facedown on a clean, light paper surface.

Place a hot, dry iron flat on the transfer for five seconds. Do not move iron around. Pick up iron and place on another area of transfer until all areas have been ironed. Lift a corner of the paper to ensure proper transfer of design.

Making a Paper Pattern for Appliqué

To make a paper pattern for appliqué, cut desired design from book. Cut around any tiny details.

Place transfer facedown on a piece of plain white paper. Transfer image; lift original transfer; set aside for future use. Mark an X on each segment of transferred image. Cut along outer edges of design lines with scissors, creating individual pattern pieces.

Place each piece on the paper side of bonded fabric, X side up (or X side down to reverse the finished image). Trace around each piece with pencil; cut out with scissors; remove paper backing.

Transferring Onto Wood

Many painted surfaces will be damaged by the heat necessary to transfer iron-on ink onto the surface.

To transfer, cut the chosen iron-on transfer from the book. Have a mirror-image photocopy made (see Tips for Using Iron-On Patterns) if the finished image needs to be pointing opposite of the transfer.

Place a sheet of graphite paper between the surface and the design; trace design lines with pointed pencil, ball-point pen or stylus. This transfers the image onto painted wood without causing paint to blister or peel. Use light-colored graphite for dark painted surfaces; use dark-colored graphite for light painted surfaces.

General Materials List

Crafters use a wide variety of supplies, tools and equipment when they are creating projects. Each of the projects in this book includes a materials list for making the design shown.

In addition you will find the following helpful in creating and adapting other Sunbonnet iron-on transfer projects:

- Low-temperature glue gun
- Scissors: sewing and pinking shears
- Paintbrushes: flat, round and wide foam
- Sponge
- Paper towels
- Paper plates
- Toothpicks
- Toothbrush
- Sewing machine
- Hand-sewing needle and thread
- Fusible sheets
- Colored pencils and markers
- Cardboard or poster board
- White paper
- Staple gun
- Hammer
- Sawtooth hangers
- Wire cutters and heavy-gauge wire
- Sandpaper: coarse and fine

Design Techniques

Toothpick Roses

Practice placing one dot light and one dot dark paint side by side (almost touching) on a piece of scrap paper.

Insert the point of a toothpick in the light dot and swirl in a clockwise direction one or two times to mix paint together slightly, like petals on a rose.

Allow paint to dry.

Add leaves, tiny white dots for baby's breath, etc.

Heart Flowers

Place two dots of same-color paint side by side. Join dots at the base by pulling one dot into the other into a point. Practice several times on scrap paper until the technique feels comfortable.

Add leaves at base of heart by squeezing a dot of green paint and drawing it to a point with the bottle tip, brush or toothpick.

Making a Padded Shape

Cut a piece of cardboard, mat board or tagboard into the desired size and shape. It is easiest to create smooth corners when they have been rounded.

Cut a piece of fabric 2" larger than cardboard shape. Cut a piece of quilt batting the same size as the cardboard shape.

Glue batting to one side of cardboard.

Transfer iron-on in center of fabric; decorate as desired; center image on batting side of cardboard.

Wrap fabric around batting to cardboard side. Tack in place with dots of glue. Smooth corners; glue in place all around periphery.

Trim any excess fabric.

Apply piping or lace insert.

Glue shape in position on surface. If trim is finished along both long edges, glue on now to cover seam between surface and padded shape.

Tips for Using Iron-On Patterns

Transfer markers

The ink on iron-on transfers will produce good, sharp images for only a finite number of transfers. When the transferred image becomes faint, revive it by marking over design lines with a transfer pen or pencil. These are available in craft, fabric and quilting stores.

Ironing on photocopied images

Freshly photocopied images are iron-on transfers in disguise. Simply position the photocopied image onto the surface, ink side toward the surface. Apply dry heat appropriate for the surface with firm pressure.

This works best on light surfaces with a photocopy less than 48 hours old—the fresher, the better the transfer. Just remember, the transferred image will be a mirror image of what you see. To change orientation, see below.

Changing the size of the iron-on transfer image

Most copy centers, libraries, business centers, printers and office-supply stores have photocopy machines that can enlarge or reduce the size of any motif. Ask them to copy the transfer at a percentage of the original (anything larger than 100 percent will enlarge the image; anything smaller than 100 percent will reduce it). The image may then be transferred to your chosen surface using one of the methods described.

Changing the orientation of the iron-on transfer image

If figures and motifs (not words) are pointing the wrong direction for your project, take the transfer to a copy center or business center. Most will have a photocopy machine that can print a mirror image of the original. The image may then be transferred to your chosen surface using one of the methods described.

Another way to flip the images is to place the transfer on the surface, image side up. Slip a piece of graphite or dressmaker's carbon between the surface and transfer. Trace over the design lines with a pencil or ballpoint pen to transfer the image to the surface.

Adapting the iron-on transfer shape

Iron-on transfer shapes can be changed to accommodate the desired surface, such as a square design used for a vest with doily lapels. The original design was square. To fit the design to the point of the vest, the square was cut open and rearranged on the vest. Pieces were taped together with heat-resistant tape (available in fabric and quilting stores) before the iron-on was transferred to vest.

Fabric appliqué

Almost any iron-on design may be used as a pattern for fabric appliqué. To hand-appliqué, follow directions for Making a Paper Pattern for Appliqué, but add 1/8" seam allowances all around each piece and use no fusible.

To machine-appliqué, follow directions for Making a Paper Pattern for Appliqué. Outline each piece with medium-width satin stitch in coordinating or contrasting thread.

Add details with machine or hand embroidery instead of paint or marker.

Ribbon-embroidery leaves and flowers would add interest and dimension on fabric pieces.

Wreath inserts

Almost any iron-on design can be used to make an insert for a wreath by manipulating the image to the desired size and shape, then transferring it to heavy paper or mat board. Once the design is embellished, the paper or mat board may be glued into the wreath opening.

Making cross-stitch, plastic canvas or needlepoint charts

To turn iron-on into a cross-stitch, plastic canvas or needlepoint pattern, photocopy iron-on at 200 percent, then copy again onto graph paper. Color squares with colored pencils. Work on even-weave fabric, such as Aida cloth, using design colored with colored pencils as a chart.

Words may be added or deleted, as desired. Simply cut words out of iron-on before applying heat to transfer design.

Paintbrushes

When using paint for your iron-on, different types of paintbrushes are necessary to achieve a neat finish.

A large area should be painted with a flat paintbrush. A small, round paintbrush works best to get into tight, detailed areas, and a wide foam brush works best for glazing.

Colored pencils

When working with colored pencils, colors may be shaded to give the image depth, but it is difficult to add highlights with a lighter pencil. Work with lightest pressure on pencil in areas where sunlight would touch the design; use heaviest pressure where shadows would fall.

Adding glitter

To add glitter to fabric designs, use a glitter paint or sprinkle dry (garment-grade) glitter on while paints or dyes are still wet. Shake excess glitter onto a piece of paper that has been folded and opened up again. Use the fold to funnel glitter back into bottle for future use.

Add glitter to designs on paper by applying a light coat of glue (appropriate for the surface) in desired area; sprinkle glitter on. Press lightly with fingers to set glitter in glue. Dry; return excess glitter to the bottle for future use.

Make several photocopies, then experiment

Don't be afraid to experiment. Make several photocopies for just a few pennies. These can be cut up and rearranged many times until the design is just right for your project. Then cut the iron-on transfer and arrange it like the photocopies before transferring the image onto the desired surface.

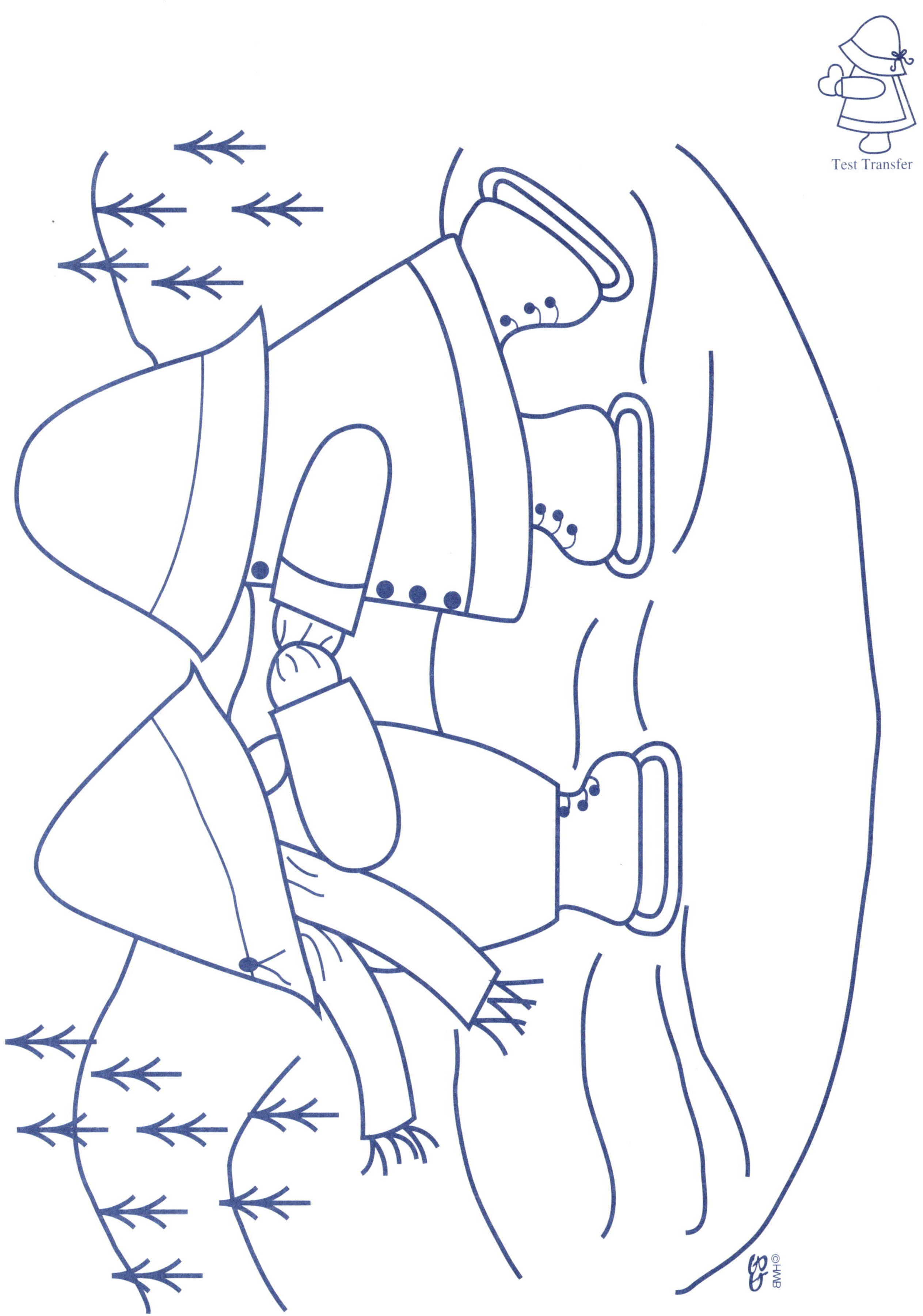
Test Transfer

LET IT SNOW !

©HWB

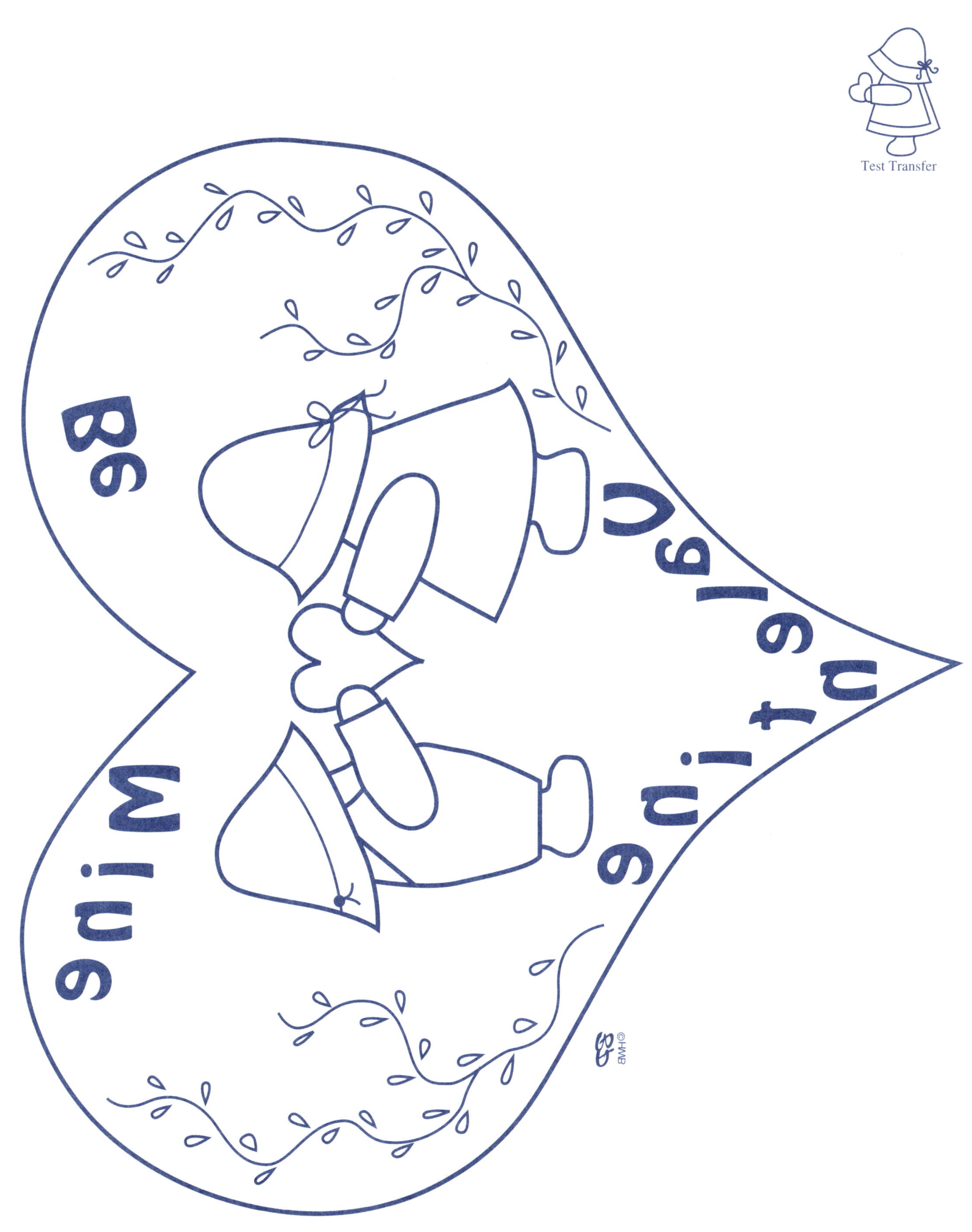
Test Transfer

Test Transfer

Roses Are Red
Violets Are Blue
Sending These
Angels To
Watch Over You

©HWB

Roses Are Red
Violets Are Blue
Sending These
Angels To
Watch Over You

Test Transfer

Test Transfer

Absence Makes the Heart Grow Fonder

Test Transfer

Test Transfer
HOME IS WHERE YOU HANG
YOUR HEART

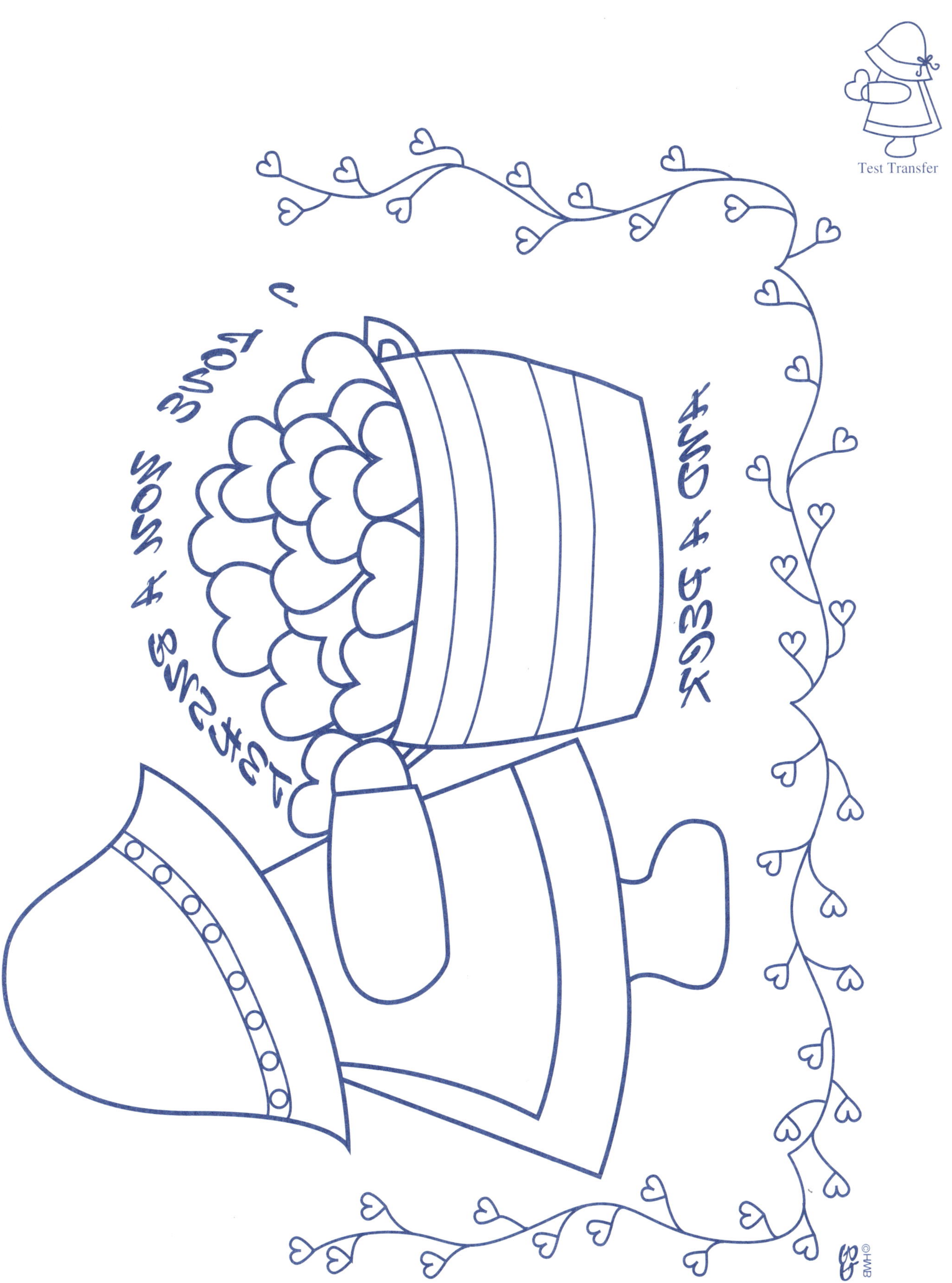
Test Transfer

Test Transfer

Test Transfer

When This You See

Remember Me

Test Transfer

Kiss Me I'm Irish

Happy Easter

Test Transfer
It's Raining Violets

Rain Rain Go Away

Test Transfer
April Showers Bring May Flowers

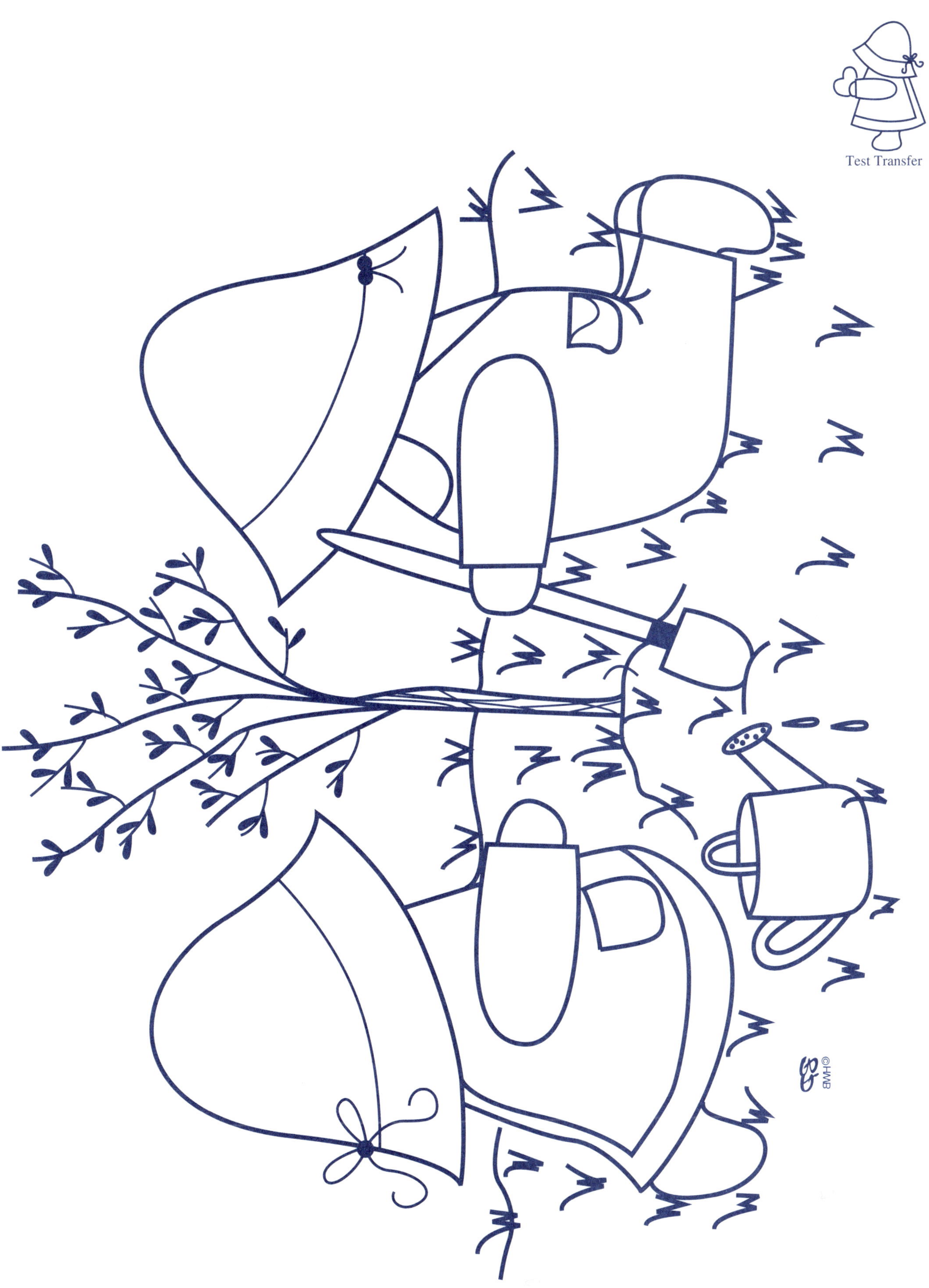
Test Transfer

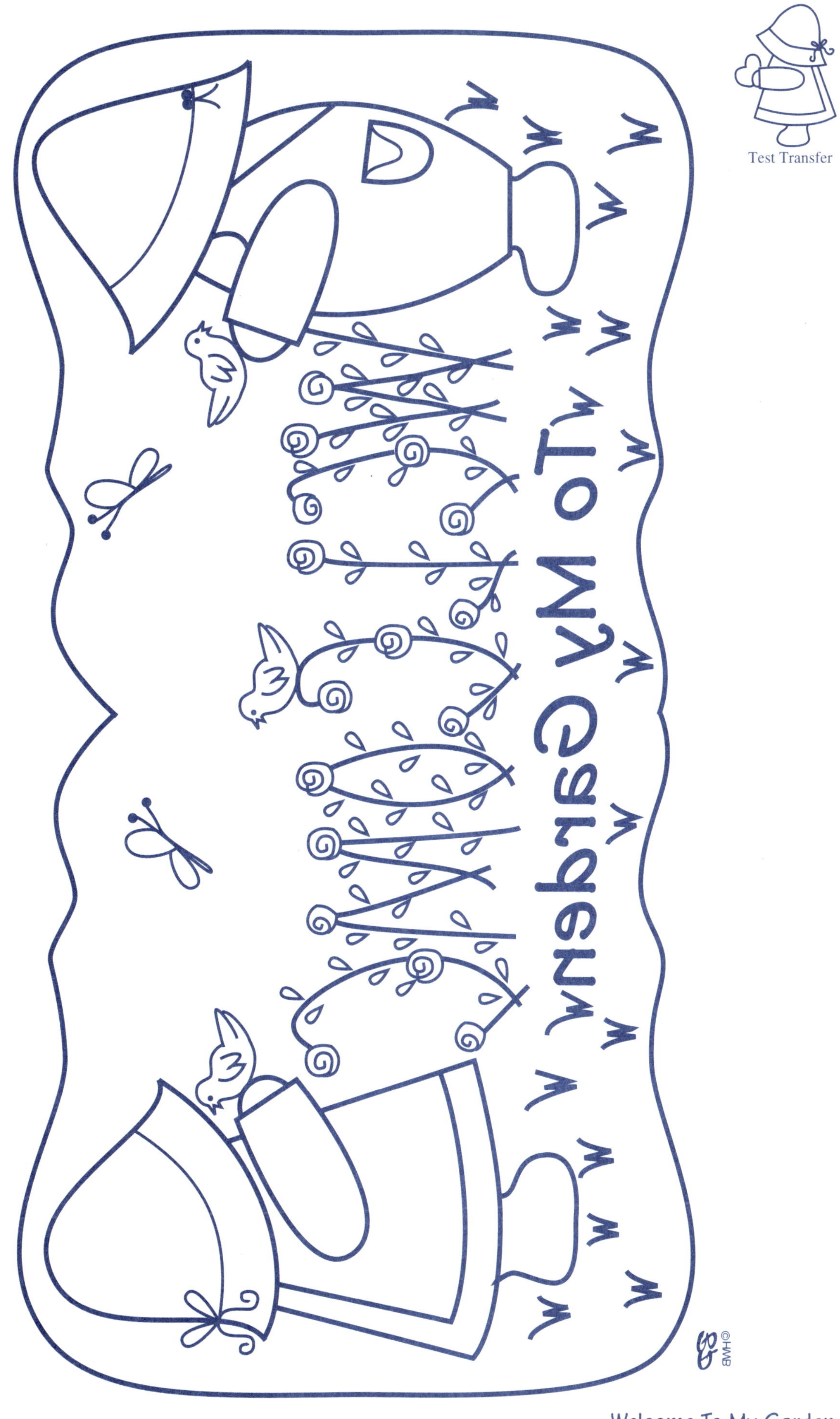
Test Transfer

Test Transfer

She Who Plants A Garden

Plants Happiness

©HWB

Time Began In a Garden

Time Began In a Garden

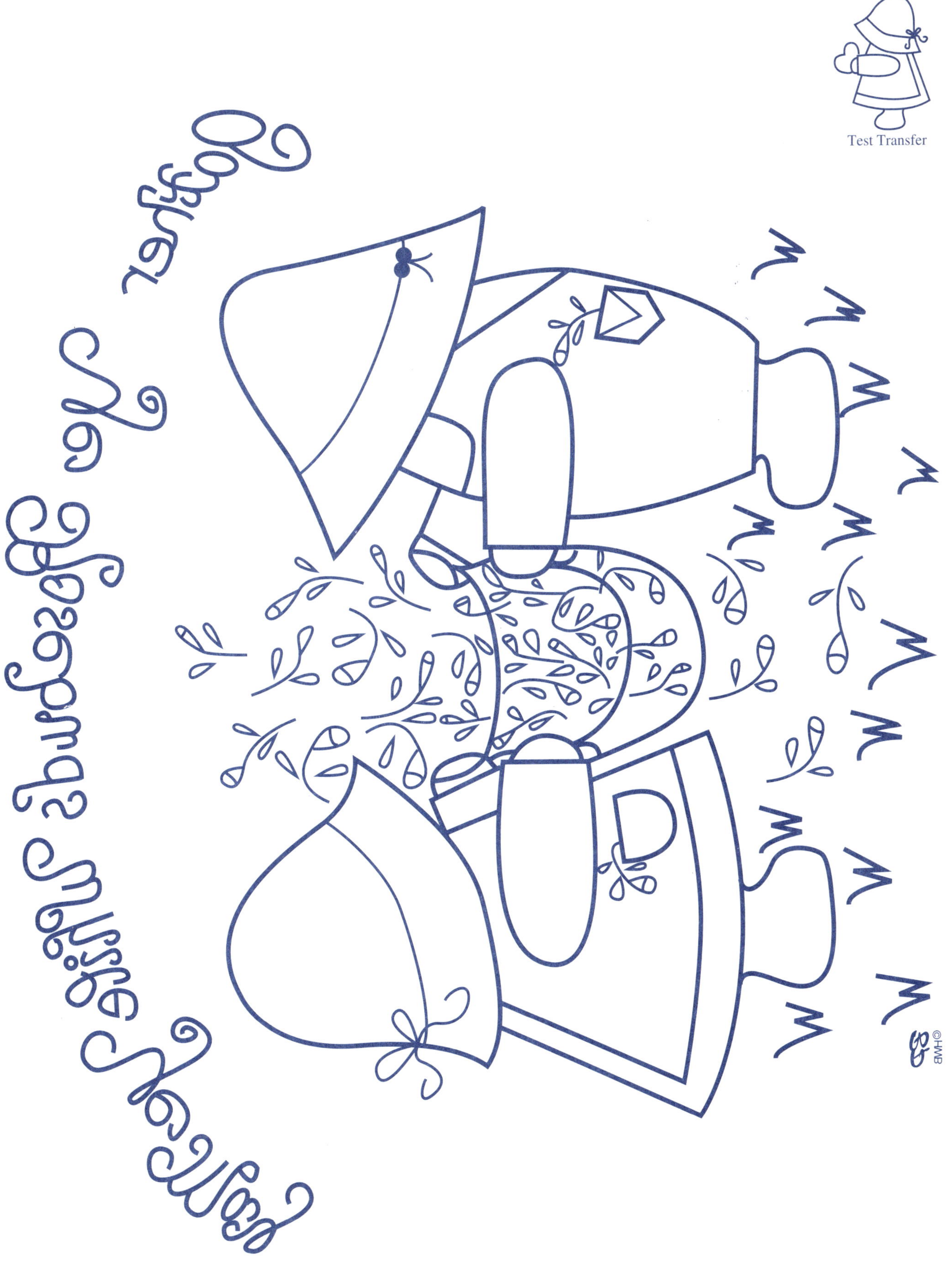
Test Transfer

Test Transfer

I LOVE YOU

MOM

©HWB

I Love You Mom

Test Transfer

I Love You Dad

Test Transfer

Let's Get Hitched

Test Transfer

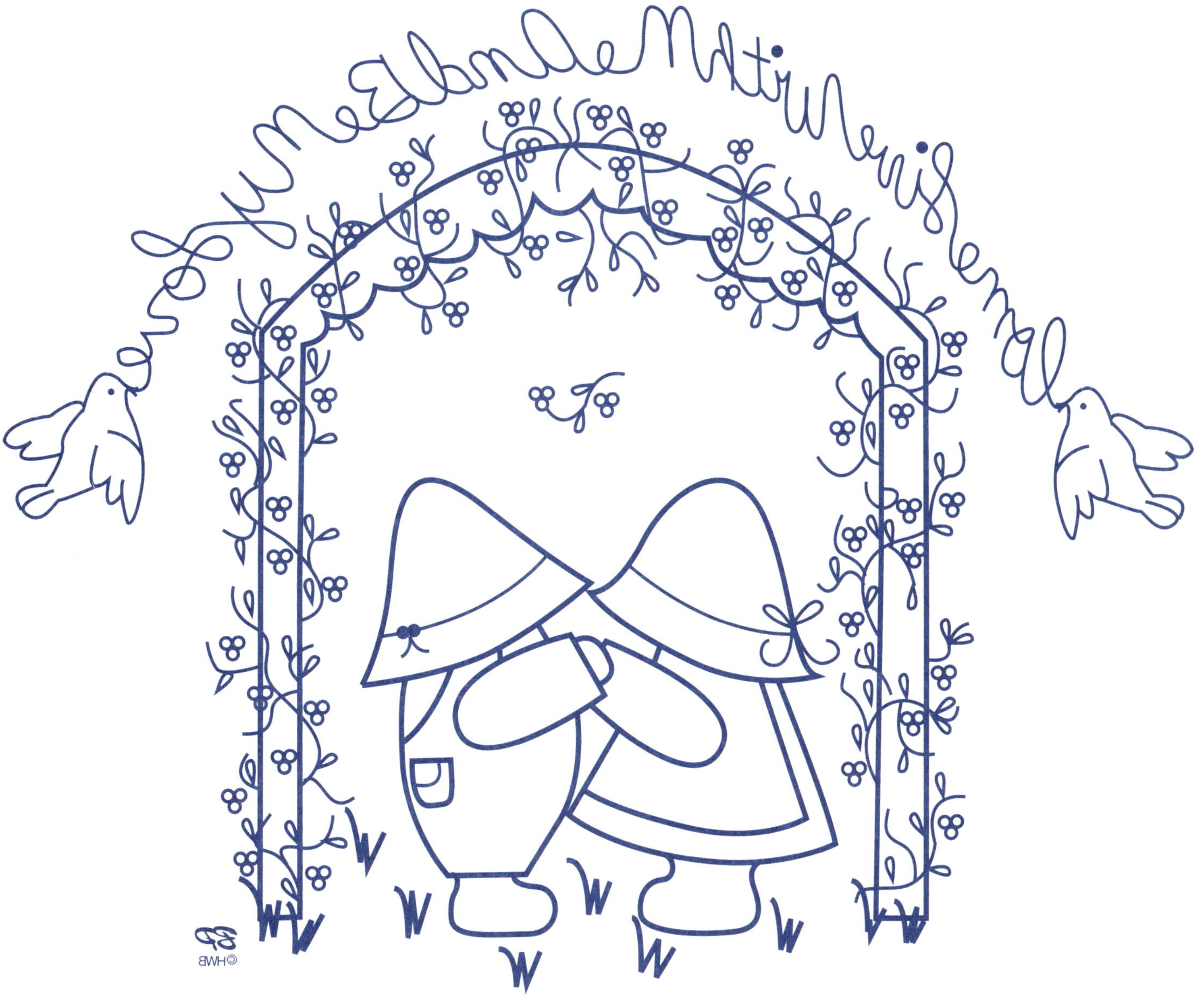

SUE & SAM

JUNE 1, 1997

Come Live With Me And Be My Love

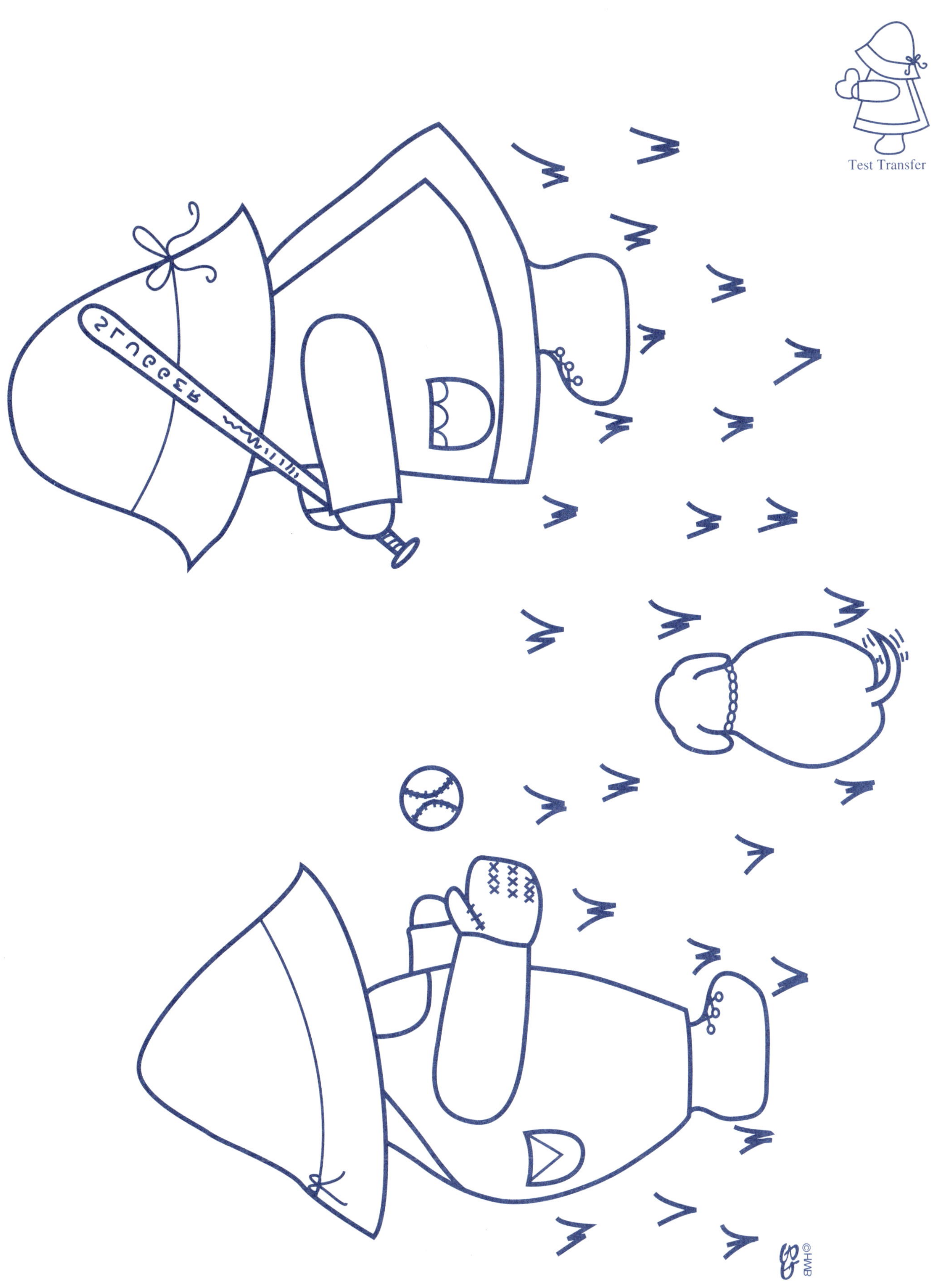
Test Transfer

Test Transfer

God Bless America

Test Transfer

♡ Friends Forever ♡

©BWH

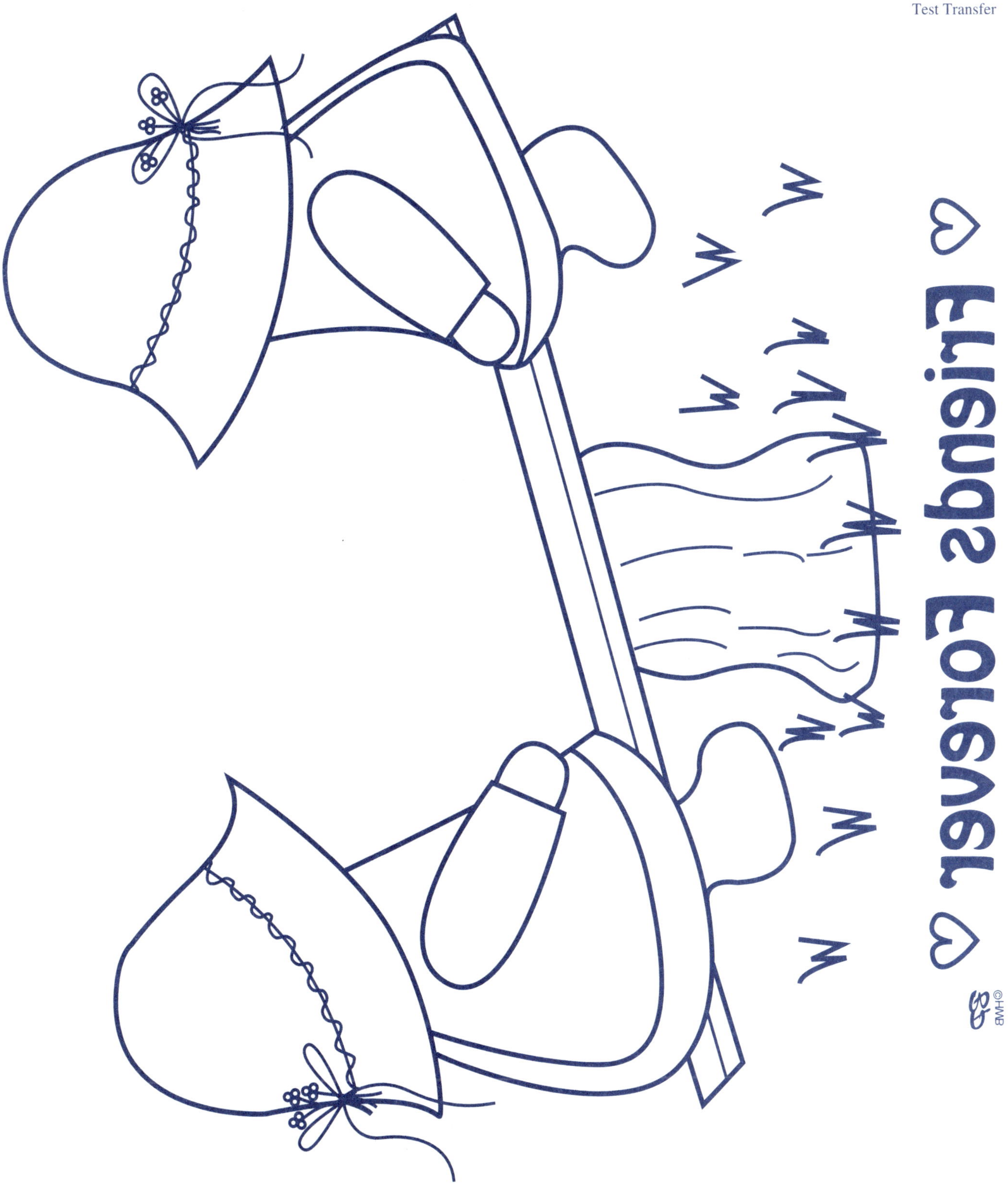

Test Transfer

Test Transfer

Test Transfer

Go Team

Test Transfer

Test Transfer

Merry Christmas

MERRY CHRISTMAS

MERRY CHRISTMAS

©HWB

Test Transfer

I'm a Little Angel

©HWB

Test Transfer

Test Transfer

Test Transfer

March

Test Transfer

May

June

July

Test Transfer
August

Test Transfer

September

Test Transfer

November

Test Transfer

Test Transfer

Sunday

Test Transfer

Monday

Test Transfer

Test Transfer

Wednesday

Test Transfer

Thursday

Test Transfer

Friday

Test Transfer

Saturday

Test Transfer

Happy Birthday

Test Transfer
Happy Birthday

Test Transfer

Test Transfer

Test Transfer

QUILTERS ARE

PIECE-MAKERS

Test Transfer

It Comforts Me And
Warms My Heart
My Quilt And I
Shall Never
Part

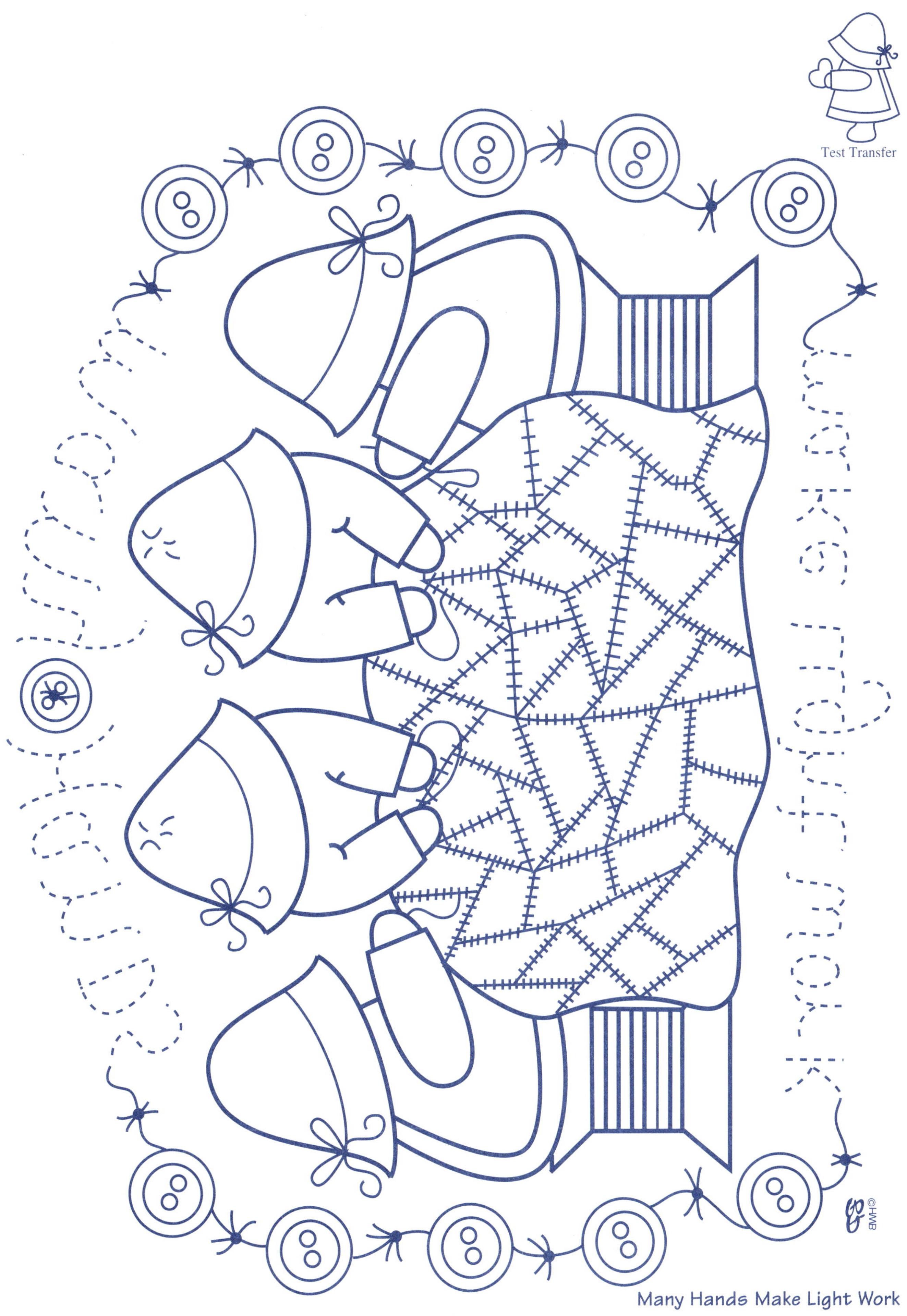

Many Hands Make Light Work

Test Transfer

Once upon a time

Test Transfer

When You Wish Upon A Star

Keep A Song In Your Heart

And You'll Never Grow Old

Keep A Song In Your Heart
And You'll Never Grow Old

Make A Joyful Noise

Test Transfer

Would This Garland Fair
Might Weave Around This Life
A Spell To Shield From Care
A Guard From Every Strife

Test Transfer

A Spoonful of Sugar Helps The Medicine Go Down

Sugar And Spice And Everything Nice
That's What Little Girls Are Made Of

Snips And Snails And Puppy Dog Tails
That's What Little Boys Are Made Of

One Toy Dispels A Hundred Cares

Test Transfer

Test Transfer

Kiss The Cook

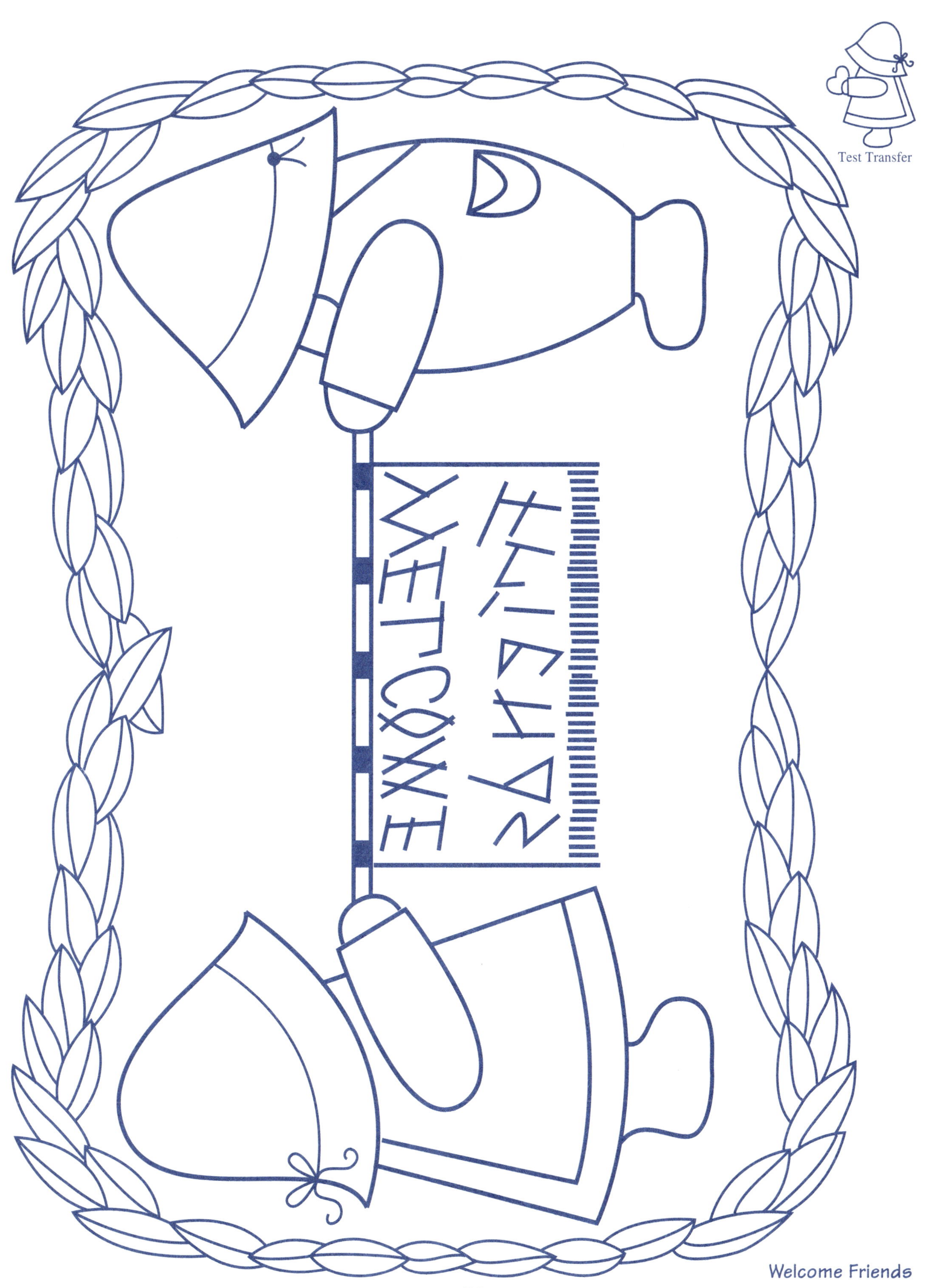
Test Transfer
WELCOME
FRIENDS

Test Transfer

To Share With A Friend Is To See Twice The Beauty

Test Transfer

IF FRIENDS WERE FLOWERS

I'D PICK YOU

Test Transfer

Test Transfer

TEA FOR
TWO
FRIENDS
SO
TRUE

Test Transfer

Test Transfer

Pleasant Words Are Like A Honeycomb

©HWB

East Or West Home Is Best

Test Transfer

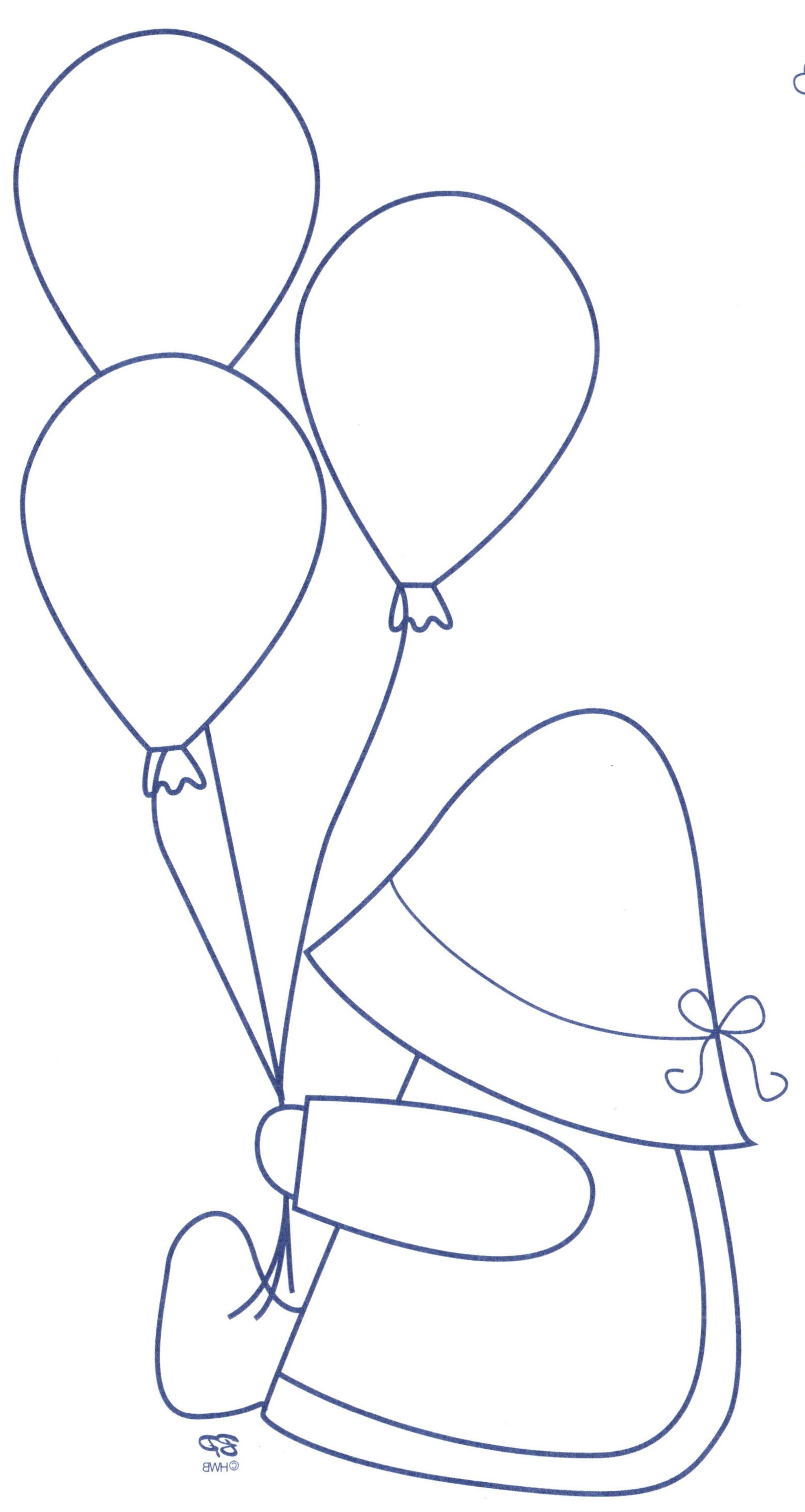

Test Transfer

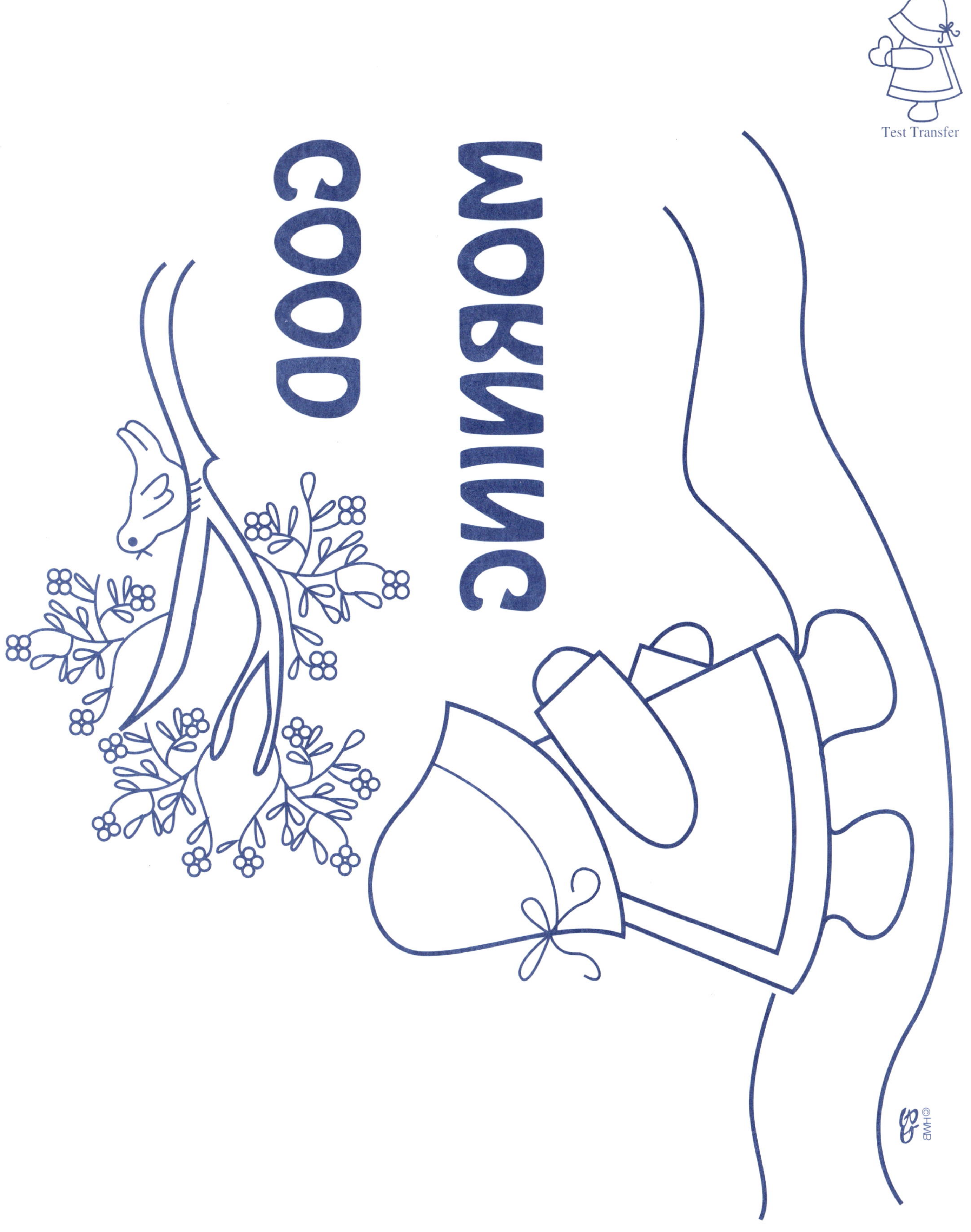
Test Transfer
GOOD
MORNING
©HWB

GOOD
NIGHT

Test Transfer

Test Transfer

Test Transfer

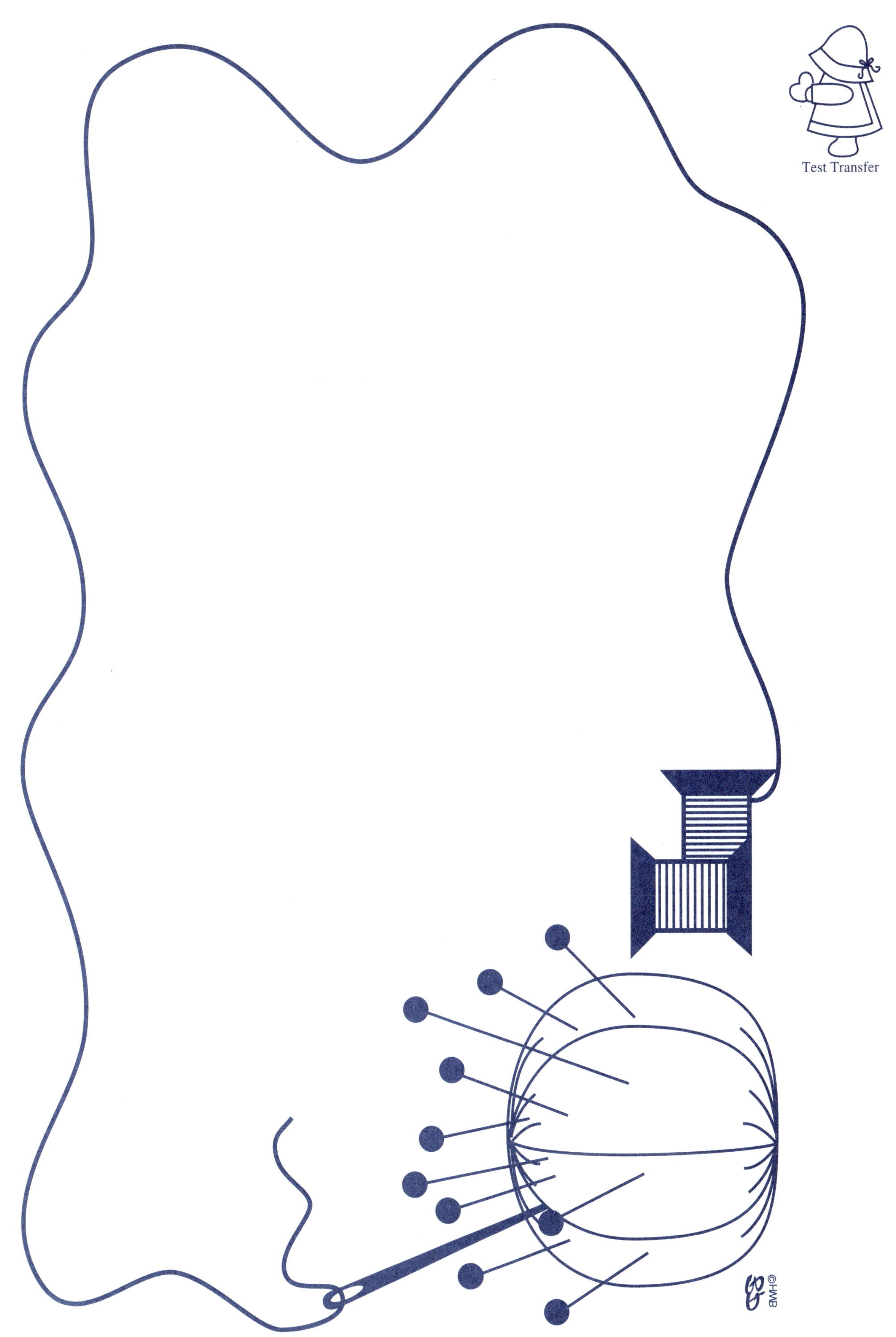
Test Transfer
©HWB

Test Transfer

Test Transfer
©HWB

Test Transfer

Test Transfer

Test Transfer

Test Transfer

A B C D E F G H I

J K L M N O P Q

R S T U V W X Y Z

1 2 3 4 5 6 7 8 9 0

A B C D E F G H I

J K L M N O P Q

R S T U V W X Y Z

1 2 3 4 5 6 7 8 9 0

i h g f e d c b a

r q p o n m l k j

z y x w v u t s

i h g f e d c b a

r q p o n m l k j

z y x w v u t s

i h g f e d c b a

r q p o n m l k j

z y x w v u t s

i h g f e d c b a

r q p o n m l k j

z y x w v u t s